kid cook book

The next stage babycook book. 25 recipes to encourage your children to eat fruit and vegetables.

Contents

Yummy homemade sauces!

Yummy vegetables!

Yummy fruit!

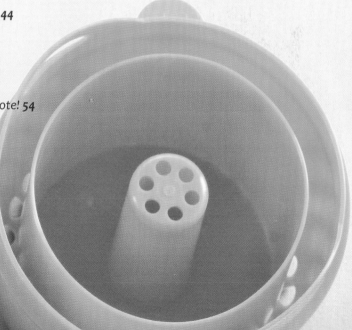

Virginie's basic rules

Eat 5 servings of fruit and vegetables a day!

Who of you have ever had to put up with a sulking child absolutely refusing to eat what you have so lovingly prepared? That's yucky! I don't like it! I don't want it! Our arguments aren't always convincing and we quickly lose our patience, especially after a hard day at work.

I'm a full-time mother of 3, designer and cookbook writer. This triple experience over the years has enabled me to amass the tricks that have given rise to this book.

Here are 25 recipes that will help you to cook nutritious, easy-to-prepare and easy-to-eat dishes for your children!

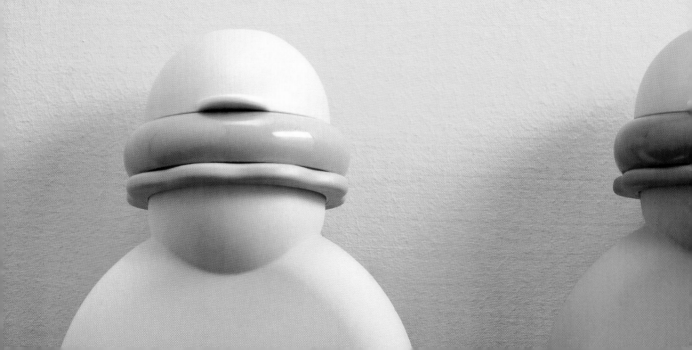

1. Always bear in mind that kids love what they can eat with their fingers. They also love a colorful, playful and surprising presentation and miniatures.

2. Set yourself up like a professional with essential, time-saving equipment, which you will find at shopping malls, over the Internet, at specialty retailers and even at Swedish furniture stores:
• A babycook®, naturally, for cooking, mixing and blending • A melon baller for making little balls • An Alligator® vegetable dicer for making uniform little cubes • A small mandolin for slicing very finely • An apple corer for making holes • A vegetable peeler for fun effects that always leave a good impression • Original ice trays and cake molds in silicone • Pastry cutters for making shapes • A syringe for making drawings on soups • Wooden sticks for making ice pops and lollipops • Colored superfine sugar

3. Be creative; make your children participating artists; speak to them about colors rather than ingredients; camouflage what they don't like inside a figure or an ingredient they love; use fresh or frozen vegetables; steam them for a short time so they stay crisp and finish them off in a frying pan with a drizzle of olive oil. It makes a big difference!

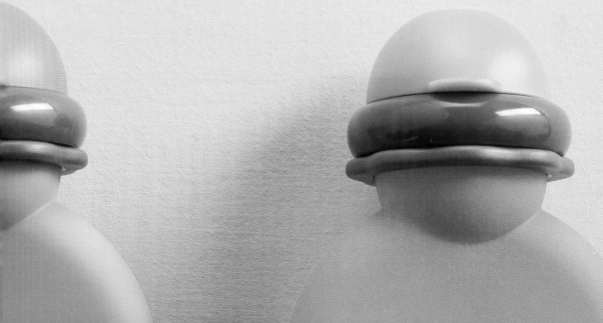

Béaba and babycook

After its founding in 1989, Béaba immediately began appealing to mothers in search
of high-quality, easy-to-use and innovative products with a contemporary design.
When this French company launched babycook, it revolutionized the world of childcare.
This food processor that steams, blends, defrosts and reheats lets you prepare meals for
babies in under 15 minutes, making it an essential for countless moms.
The babycook range has since grown to include: babycook seasoning balls, the babycook
pasta/rice cooker, babypote, maxi and baby portion sets, the evoluclip training cup,
multiportions, the lunchbox, the babycook scale... and the babycook bag so you can take
your babycook anywhere!

Further information at www.beaba.com.

Babycook accessories

babycook seasoning ball

babycook pasta/rice-cooker

babypote

maxi and baby portion sets

evoluclip training cup

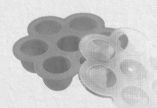

multiportions

lunch box

babycook bag

babycook scale

Yummy
homemade sauces!

Red sauce

Here's a sauce that hides its good intentions well! It contains several vegetables and is ideal for accompanying pasta, rice, cereal or meat. For a homemade Bolognese sauce, add a little ground meat.

For 20.3 fl oz (2 maxi portion containers)

1 clove of garlic • 1.75 oz zucchini • 1.75 oz eggplant • 1/2 purple onion • Olive oil •
4 cherry tomatoes • 2 tbsp tomato paste • 14 oz canned crushed tomatoes •
The leaves from 4 sprigs of basil • Salt and pepper

1. Weigh out the ingredients. Peel and crush the garlic and place it in a seasoning ball.

2. Dice the zucchini, eggplant and onion. Use 2 measures of water and steam them for 10 minutes in your babycook with the seasoning ball.

3. For the more adventurous among you, finish the cooking in a frying pan (without garlic) for 5 minutes with a tablespoon of olive oil.

4. Pour the contents of the pan back into the babycook with the rest of the ingredients. Chop finely, depending on the desired consistency. Add salt and pepper to taste.

Dips

When it comes to snacks, kids love joining in and having fun with food, especially if it's brightly colored. Easy to make and nutritionally balanced, these dips are a treat for them! Blend all the ingredients together and serve the dip with raw vegetables (cucumber, zucchini, carrot, cherry tomato, Belgian endive and radish), with potato chips or with cocktail sausages.

For about 5 fl oz (1 baby portion container)

1. Green dip • 1/2 avocado • The leaves from 4 sprigs of cilantro • The juice from 1/2 lemon

Blend.

2. Yellow dip • 1 small can (5.25 oz) corn (GMO-free) • 1 tbsp fromage frais or Greek yogurt

Rinse and drain the corn. Blend it with the fromage frais and strain through a sieve.

3. Pink dip • 1.75 oz beet • 1.75 oz feta cheese • 1 tsp olive oil

Blend.

4. Orange dip • 1 clove of garlic • 1 small red bell pepper • Olive oil • 3 cherry tomatoes

Peel and crush the garlic and place it in a seasoning ball. Use a vegetable peeler to remove the skin from the pepper and dice. Use 1 measure of water and steam it for 6 minutes in your babycook with the seasoning ball. Finish the cooking (without garlic) in a small frying pan with 1 tbsp of olive oil. Pour the contents of the pan back into the babycook with the tomatoes and blend.

Green sauce

This sauce is really a pesto, which makes it ideal to accompany pasta. Choose the most playfully shaped pasta: bows, fusilli or miniature pasta shapes... You can find pasta in all sorts of shapes and colors in supermarkets!

For about 2.5 fl oz (1/2 baby portion container)

1 large bunch of fresh basil (1 oz) • 1.75 oz unshredded fresh Parmesan cheese • 2 tbsp very good quality olive oil

1. Pluck the leaves from the basil. Cut the Parmesan into cubes.

2. Blend the leaves and cheese in your babycook with the olive oil. You will need to open the machine once or twice to scrape down the sides as the basil tends to stick to them.

Yummy
vegetables!

Yellow corn cream

This cream soup is quick to make and has the slightly sugary flavor that kids love. It's also delicious with mozzarella balls that melt in the hot soup.

For 1 child

1 medium can (10.5 oz) corn (GMO-free) • 1 shallot or 1 small onion • A little olive oil and salted butter • 1 bouillon cube • 1 pinch of paprika • Some salted popcorn • Salt and pepper

1. Dice the shallot (or onion) into small cubes. Place the shallot in a small frying pan with a little olive oil and warm on low heat without browing until it softens.

2. Rinse the corn and put it in a saucepan with the bouillon cube and the shallot. Add enough cold water to cover the corn and bring to a boil. Once it boils, pour the contents of the saucepan into the babycook.

3. Blend until you obtain a smooth cream. Strain it through a sieve while pushing with a spoon to recover as much as possible. Add salt and pepper to taste.

4. Sprinkle the paprika and popcorn over it and serve it hot with a drizzle of olive oil or a tbsp of salted butter.

Little green man flying saucer soup

This soup contains a lot of vitamins and can be adapted to other green vegetables. The little cheese flying saucers are perfect for this recipe and allow the soup to be sweetened. If you wish, you can place the figure of an alien in the middle to your children's delight.

For 1 child

1 large zucchini (18 oz) • 1/2 chicken bouillon cube •
2 cheese disks, such as Mini Babybel® • Salt and pepper

1. Peel and slice the zucchini.

2. Place the zucchini slices in a saucepan with enough water to cover them and add the bouillon cube. Cook for 5 minutes counting from the moment it starts to boil.

3. Drain the zucchini and reserve the cooking liquid.

4. Blend it very finely in your babycook with one cheese disk. Add a little liquid depending on the desired consistency. Add salt and pepper if required.

5. Serve hot with the other cheese disk in the center.

Halloween soup

Put a little coconut milk in a syringe and have fun drawing little figures depending on the event or time of year. Or ask your child to do it... Success guaranteed!

For 2 children

18 oz pumpkin • 1 tsp coarse salt • 3.5-5 fl oz (1/2-2/3 cup) canned coconut milk (or crème fraîche) • Salt and pepper

1 syringe for decorating

1. Peel the pumpkin, remove the seeds and cut into cubes.

2. Put it in a saucepan with the coarse salt. Add enough cold water to cover the pumpkin and bring to a boil. Cover the saucepan and leave it to cook for 30 minutes over medium heat.

3. Blend everything in the babycook until you obtain a smooth cream. Add the coconut milk and blend again. Add salt and pepper to taste.

4. Serve hot.

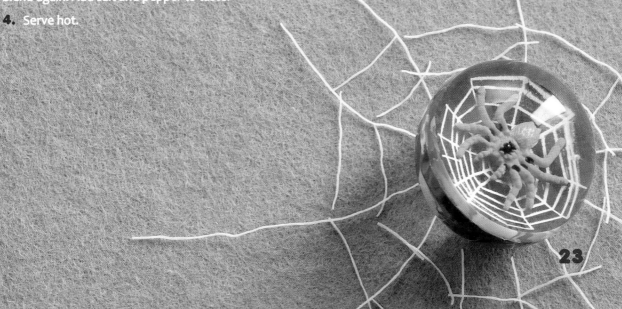

Mini toasted sandwiches

Let your child participate in putting these little toasted sandwiches together. This is a fun and easy activity because everything is small.

Save the leftover red pepper for a dip recipe, that way your child will discover the sweet flavour of crunchy peppers.

For 1 child (2 mini toasted sandwiches)

4 slices of Melba toast rounds • 1 small red bell pepper • 1 small green bell pepper • 1 clove of garlic • Olive oil • A few fresh basil leaves • 1 slice of ham • 2 Mini Babybel® cheese disks in the flavour of your choice • 2 quail eggs or small chicken eggs

Use a vegetable peeler to remove the skin from the bell peppers. Cut them into thick slices then trim them to obtain 4 circles (2 red and 2 green) with the same diameter as the Melba toast rounds. Peel and crush the garlic and place it in a seasoning ball.

Place the 4 pepper circles and the seasoning ball in your babycook, use 3 measures of water and steam them for 20 minutes.

Discard the garlic after cooking. Dry the pepper circles on paper towel before marinating them in a little olive oil infused with chopped basil.

In the meantime, cut the ham slice in two halves. Cut each Mini Babybel® disk in half to obtain 4 disk-shaped portions.

24

5. Take 1 Melba toast round and stack 1 Mini Babybel® disk, 1/2 ham slice folded in two, 1 marinated green pepper circle, 1 marinated red pepper circle, another Mini Babybel® disk and another Melba toast round over it. Do the same with for the other toasted sandwich.

6. Heat the sandwiches in a sandwich maker or in the oven until the cheese is melted.

7. While you are waiting, heat a non-stick frying pan and fry the two quail or small chicken eggs that will go on top of the sandwiches. Serve immediately.

Pasta time!

This recipe is very simple to make and can be adapted to what you have in your pantry. A tip for moms in a hurry: don't think twice about using frozen cut vegetables. A handful of each and presto!

For a salad version, use multicolored fusilli and add a few basil leaves and a little feta cheese. Kids will really love this colorful salad.

For 1 child

3 oz spaghetti or linguine • A little coarse salt • 5 small asparagus spears • 10 snow peas • 1 handful of fresh or frozen peas (not canned!) • 10 round slices of a small zucchini • Olive oil • 1 handful of red and yellow cherry tomatoes • Parmesan cheese shavings • Salt and pepper

1. Cook the pasta with a little coarse salt for the time indicated on the package.

2. In the meantime, cut off the bottom half of the asparagus. Cut the tips in half lengthways.

3. Use 1 measure of water and steam the green vegetables together in your babycook for 2 minutes (they have to remain crisp). Sauté them for 2 minutes in a frying pan with a little olive oil.

4. Cut the tomatoes into halves.

5. Mix the pasta with all the vegetables. Drizzle with a little olive oil and decorate with Parmesan shavings. Add salt and pepper to taste.

Omelet Lego

The trick here is to use pastry molds with original shapes to make a really simple vegetable omelet. You can replace the zucchini with another vegetable you might have at hand: mushroom, eggplant or bell peppers, for instance.

Cooked in a cake mold and cut into cubes, this omelet will be enjoyed by the whole family as a snack.

For 1 child

1 zucchini • 2 large onions • Olive oil • 2 eggs • 1.75 oz shredded cheese • Salt and pepper

1. Cut the zucchini into slices without peeling. Peel and slice the onions. Blend everything together in your babycook to obtain a coarse-textured purée.

2. Cook this mixture in a non-stick frying pan over low heat with 1 tbsp of olive oil until all the water evaporates. Leave to cool.

3. Beat the eggs. Add the cooked vegetables, the shredded cheese and salt and pepper.

4. Pour the omelet into your child's favourite mold and bake for 15-20 minutes at 350°F.

5. Remove it from the mold and serve warm or cold with a few lettuce leaves.

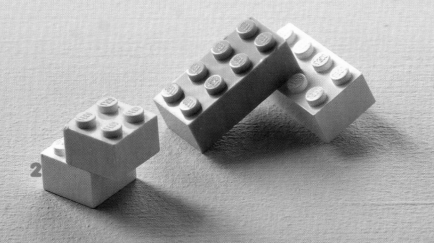

Purée jigsaw

You don't have time to prepare a homemade purée? The idea is to prepare different-colored vegetable purées in advance and store them in the freezer in fun ice trays. When it's meal time, your child can choose the colors and shapes he or she feels like. You just take them out of the tray, put them on a plate, warm them in the microwave for a few seconds and there you are!

Ingredients (of your choice)

50% potato (variety for making mashed potato) and 50% vegetables

Vegetables to choose depending on the desired color:
- Viteloutte (purple) potatoes for pink purée • Carrots for orange purée
- Chestnuts for brown purée • Broccoli for green purée
- Cauliflower for white purée • A little salted butter or crème fraîche • Salt and pepper

1. Boil the potatoes. In the meantime, steam your chosen vegetables in your babycook or boil them.

2. Blend everything together in your babycook to obtain a smooth purée.

3. Don't blend the potato with the vegetables or the purée will become gluey. Mash it with a fork and add it to the vegetable purée.

4. Add a tbsp of salted butter. When making vitelotte potato and chestnut purée, use crème fraîche instead of butter because their texture is drier. Add salt and pepper to taste.

5. Serve hot.

Carrot's cube

This recipe isn't difficult and will take about 15 minutes to prepare. Here I've chosen a 100% vitamin cocktail with carrots and orange juice. You can also vary your combinations (carrots, apples and feta cheese, for instance) or even use already diced ingredients that you can find in shops.

Keep any excess vegetables for making dips.

For 1 terrine

6 large different colored carrots (white, yellow and orange) • 13.5 fl oz (1 3/4 cups) pulp-free orange juice • The leaves from 5 sprigs of cilantro • 2 envelopes (0.5 oz) powdered gelatin • Salt and pepper

1 small cake mold

1. Peel and dice the carrots (or baton them with a mandolin slicer and cut into cubes). Boil them for 10 minutes in salted water.

2. In the meantime, blend the cilantro leaves with the orange juice in your babycook. Set aside 1/2 cup of the cilantro orange juice.

3. Strain the carrots. Place them in a saucepan with the cilantro orange juice and cook for another 10 minutes until they are very tender.

4. Pour the juice that was previously set aside into a bowl. Sprinkle the powdered gelatin evenly over the surface of the liquid, allowing it to stand for about 5 minutes for the gelatin to soften.

5. Add the gelatin to the still hot (but not boiling) carrots and cilantro orange juice, stirring until they have dissolved completely. Add salt and pepper.

6 . Line the mold with plastic wrap, allowing the edges to overhang. Arrange the carrot cubes inside it. Cover them with the cilantro orange juice, leaning the mold from side to side so that it is evenly distributed.

7. Refrigerate for 3 hours. Remove it from the mold and cut it into cubes. Serve cold.

Variation: If you can't find white or yellow carrots, you can substitute organic orange carrots, which are just as delicious.

Little gourmet open sandwiches

Little gourmets will appreciate this recipe. You may want to vary the vegetables depending on the season: beans, asparagus tips, red bell peppers, corn...

You can also have fun by cutting the toast into shapes: stars, hearts, circles, anything goes!

For 1 child

1 slice wholewheat bread • 10 peas • 2 yellow cherry tomatoes • 2 red cherry tomatoes • A few baby spinach leaves • 2 radishes • 0.5 oz mature Mimolette cheese or other cow's milk cheese • 1.5 oz spreadable cream cheese

1. Use 1 measure of water and steam the peas for 2 minutes in your babycook (they have to stay crunchy). Immediately submerge them in iced water to set their color and to chill them.

2. Cut the tomatoes in halves. Wash the baby spinach. Slice the radish very finely (a mandolin slicer is ideal for this). Use a vegetable peeler to make Mimolette cheese shavings.

3. Spread the cream cheese in a thick layer over the bread.

4. Then arrange the vegetables over it together with your child, ending with the Mimolette. Admire your artwork!

Freestyle pizza

How about a pizza? This may be a good way to get children to eat ratatouille.
Choose the shape that your child will like best: a surfboard, a tartlet, a heart, a square, etc.

If you don't feel like chopping vegetables into little cubes yourself, invest in an Alligator®
vegetable dicer; it's a great time-saver for moms! It lets you cut food into little cubes, which
children love. Besides, food in little pieces cooks faster.

For 8 small surfboards

1 ready-made thin crust pizza dough • 7 oz canned crushed tomatoes • 1 small zucchini •
1/2 small eggplant • 1/2 yellow pepper • 1/2 red pepper • 1/2 peeled clove of garlic • Olive oil •
1 pinch of oregano • 1.75 oz shredded cheese • 1 packet of mini mozzarella balls • Salt and pepper

1. Strain the crushed tomatoes through a fine mesh sieve to remove the liquid.

2. Dice all the vegetables into small cubes. Slice the 1/2 garlic clove very finely. Use 2 measures of water and steam the vegetables and the garlic for 10 minutes in your babycook.

3. Heat a little olive oil in a frying pan. Add the steamed vegetables with a pinch of oregano and cook for 2 minutes.

4. Unroll the pizza dough and cut it into surfboard shapes: you should be able to make 8. Place a small amount of strained tomato, vegetables and shredded cheese on each. Decorate with 1/2 a ball of mozzarella cheese. Add salt and pepper.

5. Bake in the oven for 15 minutes at 425 °F.

6. They can be eaten hot, warm or cold.

Tomato surprise

On-the-vine cocktail tomatoes are best for this starter; halfway between a cherry tomato and a traditional tomato, this variety comes in a size that it perfect for kids. To make this dish even more fun, serve the tomato in an egg cup: once children have finished scraping off every last grain of rice with a spoon, they can eat the whole thing.

For 3 children (6 tomatoes)

2 oz (just under 1/3 cup) basmati rice • 1 pinch of salt • 6 cocktail tomatoes • 1/2 avocado •
1/2 lemon • 1 thick slice of boiled ham • 1 oz feta cheese • 1 small can (5.25 oz) corn (GMO-free) •
Olive oil • Balsamic vinegar • Salt and pepper

1. Weigh out the ingredients.

2. Introduce the rice into your babycook with 2 measures of water with a pinch of salt. Pour 3 measures of water into the reservoir of your babycook and cook the rice for 18 minutes.

3. In the meantime, cut off the tops of the tomato to form lids. Use a melon baller to empty out the tomatoes (save the pulp, for instance to make a quick and easy tomato sauce).

4. Dice the 1/2 avocado (sprinkle with lemon juice to prevent it from turning black) and the ham. Crumble the feta cheese. Rinse and drain the corn.

5. Cool the rice under cold water and drain it well.
Mix it with the avocado, ham, feta and corn.
Season this mixture with olive oil and balsamic vinegar and salt and pepper to taste. Fill the tomatoes with it and cover them with their lids.

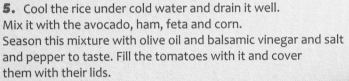

Garden party

This recipe is ideal for getting even the most reluctant kids to eat vegetables. The slightly sweet taste masks the real taste of the vegetables, but it's a surefire way I've found to get children to accept all vegetables without complaint, especially onions and turnips, from an early age. Combine these mixed vegetables with plain rice cooked in a rice-cooker and you will be surprised to see them begging for more.

For 1 child

3.5 oz frozen mixed vegetables (or a mixture of diced carrot, turnip, onion and zucchini) • 1 handful of peas • 6.75 fl oz (just over 3/4 cup) canned coconut milk • Olive oil • Salt and pepper

1. Introduce the still frozen vegetables and the peas in your babycook (without the steam basket) and add 1/4 cup of coconut milk. Fill the reservoir with 3 measures of water and cook in steam mode for 8 minutes.

2. After cooking, pour the contents of your babycook into a saucepan with 1 tsp of olive oil. Cook over medium heat until the liquid evaporates (it should have a creamy texture). Then add 1 tsp of coconut milk and mix well. Reduce the liquid again. The coconut milk should have a slightly thick consistency, like a white sauce.

3. Season with salt and pepper before serving.

Yummy
fruit!

Ice cream pop concert

This very simple recipe that relies mainly on presentation: ice trays, mini pastry molds or babycook multi-portions. Give a new use to the containers you have at home.

Condensed milk makes these ice cream pops creamy but it can also mask the flavor of the fruit. You should adjust the amount of condensed milk you use to the natural sweetness of the fruit.

For 2 classic shape ice cream pops

3.5 oz of the fresh fruit of your choice (raspberry, mango, kiwifruit, etc) • 2.5 oz of yogurt • 3-4 tbsp condensed milk (measure depending on the sweetness of your fruit)

1 original ice tray with wooden sticks or 2 classic ice pop molds

1. Weigh out your fruit. Blend it well in your babycook with the yogurt and the condensed milk.

2. Pour the fruit purée into the mold of your choice and freeze for 10 minutes. Position the sticks in the openings in the mold and return to the freezer for at least 2 hours.

Cool fruit mousse

You will find clear plastic balls on the shelves of children's entertainment and arts and crafts stores. The aim of this is for children to eat this these small mousse creations as if they were lollipops. You can also use the halves of toy capsules from vending machines, small glasses and other containers. Use your imagination!

Save the juice from this recipe to color plain Petit Suisse or yogurt.

For 10 half balls or 10 half toy capsules

5.5 oz of the fresh fruit of your choice (mango, apricot, pineapple, berries, etc.) • 3.5 oz (about 1/2 cup) fromage blanc or cream cheese • 1-2 tbsp supperfine sugar (depending on the sweetness of the fruit) • 2 egg whites • 1 pinch of salt

1. Weigh out the different fruits and blend them in your babycook. Strain the puréed fruit in a sieve to remove the excess liquid.

2. Add the fromage cheese and sugar. Mix gently.

3. Beat the egg whites with a pinch of salt until they are stiff. Fold it gently into the fruit mixture.

4. Fill the chosen containers with the mousse and refrigerate for 1 hour.

Choco chups

Here is the perfect way to get your child to eat fresh fruit. Use a favorite cake or breakfast cereal for the crumb coating.

For a festive occasion, alternate candy with the fresh fruit.

For 1 child

Fresh fruit (pear, apple, mango, kiwifruit, pineapple, etc.) • 4 bars of milk chocolate • 2 pink ladyfinger cookies

1 melon baller (to make the balls) • Lollipop sticks

1. Peel the fruit and scoop out balls with the melon baller. If you use pears, apples or bananas, sprinkle them with lemon juice to prevent them from turning dark.

2. Pierce the fruit balls with the lollipop sticks. Put them in a bowl.

3. Put the pieces of chocolate in a second bowl and microwave it for 10 seconds.

4. Crush the pink cookies into a fine powder in your babycook. Place the crumbs in a third bowl.

5. Now it's ready! Your child only has to dip a fruit lollipop in the chocolate and then in the crunchy cookie crumbs.

Caramel pear

This recipe can also be made with an apple. Peel and remove the core with an apple corer. It can also be fun to make holes all over it with an apple corer. Use 3 measures of water and steam it for 20 minutes in your babycook. Just before serving, pour the caramel sauce (this time made with apple juice) through the top hole and stick a caramel bar through the middle of the apple, as if it were a stalk.

1 Conference pear • 3 chewy caramel bars + 1 for decoration • 2 tbsp of pear nectar or milk

1. Peel the pear. Use 3 measures of water and steam it for 15 minutes in your babycook.

2. In the meantime, melt 3 caramel bars with the pear nectar (or milk) in a small saucepan over low heat.

3. Pour this sauce over the warm pear and serve immediately. Pierce the pear with a caramel bar for decoration.

Variation: If you can't find a Conference pear, you can substitute a Bartlett, Bosc or d'Anjou pear.

Polar cherry soup

The amount of sugar you need depends on how sweet the fruit is, so you will need to adjust it.

If you have any soup leftover, freeze it in ice pop molds. Try using the cherry juice ice cubes to brighten up a fruit juice of another color. It will look lovely!

For 2 children

10.5 oz (about 1 1/3 cups) pitted cherries • Granulated sugar • 3.5-5 fl oz (1/2-2/3 cup) buttermilk or plain drinking yogurt

1. Stew the cherries in a saucepan with 1 tbsp of sugar for 10 minutes.

2. Strain the cherries and introduce them into your babycook. Set the juice aside. Blend them well and refrigerate the compote. Pour the juice into an ice tray and place it in the freezer.

3. Before serving, blend the chilled cherries with the buttermilk (or drinking yogurt). Serve very cold with the juice ice cubes and a dusting of sugar.

Grenadine in my compote!

This simple compote will make a nutritious snack for your child thanks to the babypote. To reduce the acidity, add 1 Golden Delicious apple while cooking. You can replace the grenadine syrup with any other fruit syrup.

For 1 child

5.5 oz frozen rhubarb in chunks   2 tbsp grenadine syrup

1. Stew the rhubarb in a saucepan with the grenadine syrup for about 15 minutes without covering until it begins to fall apart and the liquid evaporates (rhubarb gives off plenty of water).

2. Transfer it to your babycook and blend to make a smooth compote. Taste it and add a little more syrup if it is too sour.

3. Serve warm or cold, accompanied with small ladyfingers.

Bananamania

Chocolate is a great ally to have if you want to get reluctant kids to eat fruit. You can adapt this crêpe to any fruit and serve it with a scoop of ice cream or sorbet, or vanilla Chantilly cream.

For 8 crêpes

For the crêpes batter: • 4.5 oz (1 cup) all-purpose flour• 2 eggs • 1 cup milk • A little sunflower oil

For the topping: • 8 Fressinette bananas or 4 normal bananas • 1 bar of milk chocolate

1. Measure the flour. Introduce it into your babycook with the eggs and blend for about 1 minute. Add half the milk and blend for 3 minutes before adding the remaining milk and 2 tsp of oil and blend again. Stand for 1 hour (thin the batter with a little water if needed).

2. Heat a little oil in a frying pan. Pour in 1 ladleful of batter and swirl the batter so that it covers the entire surface of the pan. Cook the crêpe until it is dry and golden then flip it over. Repeat the process for the remaining crêpes.

3. Slice the bananas. Melt the chocolate in the microwave for 15 seconds. Spread half on the crêpes and coat the banana pieces with the rest of the chocolate.

Strawberry swirls

A convenient snack to slip into your child's schoolbag together with a babypote full of compote. In order to make the egg whites good and stiff, consider using egg whites at room temperature. Another trick: to remove the parchment paper easily without damaging your beautiful cake, run a rolling pin over the paper before peeling it off.

For 1 jelly roll

For the batter: • 3 eggs • 3.5 oz (just under 1/2 cup) superfine sugar • 3.5 oz (just under 1/2 cup) all-purpose flour • 2 tsp baking powder • 1 pinch of salt • A little confectioner's sugar

For the filling: • 8 oz strawberries • 2.8 oz (about 1/3 cup) granulated sugar

1. Weigh out all the ingredients. Separate the egg whites from the yolks. Introduce the yolks and the superfine sugar into your babycook and blend until the mixture turns white. Add the flour and baking powder and blend again.

2. Beat the egg whites with a pinch of salt until they are stiff. Fold it into the egg, sugar and flour mixture gently.

3. Line a baking pan with parchment paper. Spread the batter over it in an even layer of about 1/2 inch in thickness.

4. Bake in the oven at 350 °F for 8-10 minutes.

5. In the meantime, stew the strawberries in a saucepan with the sugar for about 10 minutes over low heat until you obtain what looks like the beginnings of jelly and the juice evaporates off.

6. When the cake is cooked, unmold it onto a clean damp cloth. Peel off the parchment paper gently and spread the strawberry compote over the cake. Roll the cake and cut the ends off to make them neat. Wrap the roll tightly in plastic wrap and refrigerate.

7. Just before serving, use a sifter to sprinkle confectioner's sugar over the roll.

Pink smoothie

Smoothies are a good way of getting kids to drink the kinds of fruit they don't like by hiding them among the kinds they do. This healthy drink is ideal for breakfast or as a snack with bread and butter or cookies.

For a creamier consistency, replace the milk with fromage frais or Greek yogurt.

It is also delicious with a combination of almond milk and pear.

For 1 glass

1/2 banana • 5.5 oz (just under 3/4 cup) fresh or frozen berries (blackberries, blackcurrants, blueberries, etc.) • Milk or buttermilk • Superfine sugar (depending on the sweetness of the fruit)

1. Cut the 1/2 banana into chunks. If using frozen berries, defrost them or rinse them.

2. Blend all the fruit together in your babycook and add the milk a little at a time until you obtain the desired consistency.

3. Add sugar if needed. Serve with or without ice cubes.

Party breakfast!

Make this complete and nutritious breakfast in record time. Try combining it with all kinds of fruit and cereal. If your child doesn't like chunks, blend the (peeled) fruit directly with the fromage frais or Greek yogurt.

It is also delicious with red currants, raspberries and strawberries.

For 1 small glass

1/2 pear • 1/2 apple • 2 oz tub of plain Petit Suisse or Greek yogurt • 1 handful cereal such as Cheerios® • 1 tbsp honey or crunchy brown sugar

1. Rinse the fruit. Dice the 1/2 pear and 1/2 apple without peeling. Use 1 measure of water and steam them for about 3 minutes in your babycook. Leave to cool.

2. Tip the tub of fromage frais or Greek yogurt at the bottom of a glass and add the fruit cubes. Sprinkle cereal over it and finish with the honey (or brown sugar).

2 3 4 5 6 7 8 9 10 11 12 13 14 15

The exception that proves t

The editor's acknowledgements

Thank you
to Marie Claveau, of the Béaba Company, and to all her team for supporting us throughout the process of putting together this work;
to Françoise and Virginie for their creativity and good humor; and to Anne for her cheerful and brightly colored layout.

The author's acknowledgements

My thanks
to Éditions Culinaires, particularly to Hortense Jablonski, for having entrusted me with this project which was close to my heart;
to Françoise Nicol, my partner and talented photographer, for working with me again on this project;
to Gladys Palatin, my assistant, for her daily dose of good humor and her help during the compiling of the recipes;
to Paule Neyrat, dietitian, for her suggestions;
and to my three children and guinea pigs, Arthur, Charles and Louis, for their support, their creativity and their memorable laughter while I was writing the titles.

Special thanks go to Ressource (ressource-peinture.com) for generously providing the magnificent colors that were essential for creating the backgrounds for this book:
- Rose Poudré S47, Sérénité collection
- Vert SC 271, Couleurs Traditionnelles collection
- Bleu Syracuse, Orient Occident collection
- Mauve Jalna, Orient Occident collection

The photographer's acknowledgements

Thank you
to Hortense, my editor, for her professionalism, her availability, her listening, her trust and her smile; and to Virginie for her offbeat humor and friendly impertinence.

Collection director: Emmanuel Jirou-Najou
Editor: Hortense Jablonski
Recipe creation and design: Virginie Michelin, assisted by Gladys Palatin
Photographs: Françoise Nicol
Graphic design: Anne Chaponnay
Layout: Cillero & de Motta
Translation: Cillero & de Motta
Photoengraving: Maury Imprimeur
Partnership Manager: Alice Vasseur (alice.vasseur@alain-ducasse.com)
Printing: Printed in India, The Foundry USA
Legal deposit : 2nd quarter 2011
ISBN 13: 978-2-84123-370-0
Copyright Lec. 2011
64, rue du Ranelagh
75016 Paris
www.cookboutic.fr